Soul Food
Soul-Nourishing Devotionals
& Recipes

Volume 1

By
Daunte' Simone Gibbs

Published By

ZOË LIFE
PUBLISHING
WORDS TO LIVE BY

In Partnership with Kerruso Books

Published by:
Zoë Life Publishing
P.O. Box 871066
Canton, MI 48187 USA
www.zoelifepub.com

All Scripture quotations, unless otherwise indicated, are taken from The New King James Version (NKJV) of the Bible copyright © 1982 by Thomas Nelson, Inc. The Bible text designated (RSV) is from the Revised Standard Version of The Bible, copyright © 1946, 1952, 1971 by the Division of Christian Education of the National Council of the Churches of Christ in the USA.

Take note that the name satan and associated names are not capitalized. We choose not to give him any preeminence, even to the point of violating grammatical rules.

Author: Daunte Gibbs
Illustrator: Zoe Life Creative Team
Editor: Sarah Hess and the Zoe Life Editorial Team

First U.S. Edition Year 1st Edition was Published

Publisher's Cataloging-In-Publication Data

Gibbs, Daunte

Soul Food
Christian Devotionals designed to nourish the soul and delicious heath conscious recipes to nourish the body.

10 Digit ISBN 1-934363-88-X
13 Digit ISBN 978-1-934363-88-1

1. Christian, Recipes, Spiritually Uplifting Devotionals

For current information about releases by Author's Name or other releases from Zoë Life Publishing, visit our website: http://www.zoelifepub.com

Printed in the United States of America

#v2.3 8 23 10

Dedication

I dedicate Soul Food first and foremost to the source of my being and abilities, my Lord and Savior Jesus Christ. To my dad, Stephen Gibbs Jr., a faithful man of God through whom I learned to live for Christ and cook. Dad, I love you, God bless you, and thank you from the bottom of my heart for the generational blessing! To my mother, Wanda Mae Gibbs (1954 - 1988), without her and Dad there would be no me. Thank you, Mom, for the good seed planted in me at an early age. To my wife, Sharee' Gibbs, you love me with an unconditional love that's beyond this world. You are my best friend and I deeply love, admire, and respect you. To my son Christopher Joaquin Gibbs (Christ bearer God will establish) and your future siblings, this book is a good seed that I am sowing into each of you. I love you! Last but not least, to all my loyal readers, may God bless each of you and may heaven smile upon you!

Soul Food
Soul-Nourishing Devotionals
& Recipes

Volume 1

By
Daunte' Simone Gibbs

Table of Contents

Spring Soul Food

Summer Soul Food

Fall Soul Food

Winter Soul Food

Forewords

Behold, thou desirest truth in the inward parts: and in the hidden part thou shalt make me to know wisdom (Psalms 51:6).

Why would Daunte' Gibbs ask me to write this forward for Soul Food, when I can't boil water without scorching it? It's because even I would be able to follow these recipes.

Soul Food not only offers easy to follow precise recipes but, it's full of anointed devotionals that will bless churches, men and women of God and others hungry for the word.

The favor of God is on this anointed vessel and his precious wife, Sharee'. Loosen your spirit and your belt and allow *Soul Food* to feed you till you want no more. My prayers and blessing on all *Soul Food* readers as your spirit is fed mightily.

Bishop M. D. Spires
Founder and Overseer
Church of Atlanta Lighthouse, Inc.
Atlanta, Georgia

How I wish I had had this book years ago when I accepted Christ as my personal Savior and began to desire to grow in His word. Minister Daunte Gibbs is a man of uncompromising integrity and gifting. God has anointed Gibbs with unbelievably clear, instructive and relevant insight as he writes. As Gibbs' pastor, I have watched him grow and excel the last few years to spiritual maturity. His natural ability to cook gives a spiritual parallel of spiritual recipe's as he puts his fingers on the pulse of God as it relates to spiritual food. It is with great pleasure to endorse this book as a must-read for every Christian believer.

This book is full of practical suggestions that should make understanding the word and the voice of God at this time a lot easier to understand.

As Matthew writes in chapter 6 verse 3(NIV), *"But seek first his kingdom and his righteousness, and all these things will be given to you as well."* As you read this book, your spirit man will be nurtured and fed. As the Kingdom of God as well as the world shifts, it is imperative that we have a sure prophetic word during this end time. Matthew 5:6 states, *"Blessed are those who hunger and thirst for righteousness, for they will be filled."* This is a book that expresses universal interest for every person who desires the sincere meat of the word. Regardless of the stage of your spiritual walk, you will be blessed and strengthen as you read this book.

-Pastor L. Timothy McKibbins
Church of Atlanta Lighthouse Inc.

We are tri-part beings, spirit, soul and body. For so long we have failed to recognize and nourish all three parts, therefore leaving us out of balance. It has been said that we are what we eat. In many of our cultures, various ways of cooking and living has been handed down without question as to its origin. The bible says that God created the earth and has commanded the earth to feed man, God's highest level of creation. It is our responsibility to be good stewards over what God has given us to work with. Many of the diseases that we are being treated for, in all likelihood, can be reversed and even terminated if we would just change the way we do things.

The bible says that whatsoever we bind on earth, meaning discover, overpower, get control of, shall be bound in heaven. Daunte Gibbs challenges us from a biblical perspective on how to change the way we think about what we eat and how we prepare it. But what is most pleasurable about his offering is it's not only healthy but it's good.

Bishop Joseph A. McCargo
Senior Pastor and Founder
City of Hope International Worship Centre
President International Network of Churches,
Ministries and Businesses

Introduction

Greetings to each of you in the name of our Lord and Savior Jesus Christ!

I am honored to have this opportunity to be a vessel chosen by the true and living God our Father to release and share what He would have me say according to His mighty Word.

It is with utmost excitement and enthusiasm that I introduce to you Soul Food, Vol.1: Soul-Nourishing Devotionals and Recipes, a book that offers both food for your soul and food for your belly. As the Word of God nourishes the soul, so does good cooking. Soul food is a term used to describe a specific type of food that is derived from African-American families. It was often said that Dad, Mom, Grandma, Big Mama, Madear, or whatever you called your loved one who could "throw down" in the kitchen put their heart, love, and soul into what they cooked, hence the name soul food. Just like soul food is cooking from the heart that nourishes the natural soul, the Word of God is from His heart and nourishes the spirit being.

It was my wife who recognized my natural God-given ability to cook, joy of cooking, and nurturing spirit. She knew my cooking ability went beyond just how good my final products taste. She knew I possessed a God-given gift and made it a point to make sure I became fully aware of what I have been graciously given. Therefore, she encouraged me to utilize my gifts and offer them to the world. When my eyes were finally opened, I recognized my love and natural ability for cooking.

In addition to this, I received my call to serve in the ministry of the gospel of Jesus Christ in January of 2007. So many revelations occurred in such a short time, but one that streamlined who I am was the revelation of the gifting I carry to nurture and help not only the natural but also the spiritual soul of man. All of this began in January of 2007 but did not begin to manifest as a divinely inspired written word until December of the same year. It was at this time the Lord impressed upon me to begin writing a monthly "Soul Food..." message in collaboration with my catering business. I began my monthly "Soul Food..." article series by e-mailing it to those who expressed interest in receiving it. This group consisted of friends, family, colleagues, acquaintances, and church members. As time progressed, God once again impressed upon me to take my monthly Soul Food articles a step further. Providing insight through my wife, He led me to create *Soul Food*, a book for the four seasons of the year. For each natural season of the year, I have included soul-nourishing messages and recipes that promote spiritual thought, stir spiritual gifts, enhance family relationships through cooking, and help you establish personal relationships with God our creator. It's a double portion of nourishing for your soul and body.

So long as God leads me to release what He gives me to write, I will continue the Soul Food series. I pray that it truly nourishes each soul God intends for it to reach. To God be the glory forever!

Once again, I introduce to you in the name of our Lord and Savior Jesus Christ, Soul Food, Vol.1: Soul-Nourishing Devotionals and Recipes. Amen!

Welcome Home....

Therefore, laying aside all malice, all deceit, hypocrisy, envy, and all evil speaking, as newborn babes, desire the pure milk of the word, that you may grow thereby, if indeed you have tasted that the Lord is gracious (1 Peter 2:1-3).

Spring Soul Food

Remaining Thankful in the Face of Obstacles

The Word of God says in 1 Peter 2:1 - 5,

Therefore, laying aside all malice, all deceit, hypocrisy, envy, and all evil speaking, as newborn babes, desire the pure milk of the word, that you may grow thereby, if indeed you have tasted that the Lord is gracious. Coming to Him as to a living stone, rejected indeed by men, but chosen by God and precious, you also, as living stones, are being built up a spiritual house, a holy priesthood, to offer up spiritual sacrifices acceptable to God through Jesus Christ.

The Message Bible translates 1 Peter 2:1-5 this way:

So clean house! Make a clean sweep of malice and pretense, envy and hurtful talk. You've had a taste of God. Now, like infants at the breast, drink deep of God's pure kindness. Then you'll grow up mature and whole in God. Welcome to the living Stone, the source of life. The workmen took one look and threw it out; God set it in the place of honor. Present yourselves as building stones for the construction of a sanctuary vibrant with life, in which you'll serve as holy priests offering Christ-approved lives up to God.

Life can bring us to situations that are spiritually tough. Sometimes just as we're moving forward and progressing, we're suddenly faced with an unforeseen obstacle. Sometimes there's more than one obstacle. Even if we think we've prepared for these moments, they have a tendency to mutate into something totally different than the scenario had anticipated. If we're not cautious, on spiritual guard, and continuously in communion with God during these tough times, we can become troubled to a point that we allow our flesh to entertain the idea of maliciously attacking that obstacle. This in turn opens us to engaging in other unholy acts like deceit, hypocrisy, envy, and all evil speaking. This is reason enough to stress the vital importance of what the Word of God says in Hebrews 10:22 – 25:

Let us draw near with a true heart in full assurance of faith, having our hearts sprinkled from an evil conscience and our bodies washed with pure water. Let us hold fast to the confession of our hope without wavering, for He who promised is faithful. And let us consider one another in order to stir up love and good works, not forsaking the assembling of ourselves together, as is the manner of some, but exhorting one another, and so much the more as you see the Day approaching."

Just as newborn babies desire and need the nourishing milk from their mothers that is exclusively made for them, we should set our minds to have a likeness in appetite, desire, and need for the nourishing Word of God! And by drinking from God's infinite wholesome Word, we taste God's unmerited divine support – His grace! In doing so, we come to know Him as the living stone, the source of life! After coming into the knowledge thereof, we must present ourselves as living stones (Romans 12:1) to build up the spiritual house of the chosen destiny He has for us and become a holy priesthood so that we can offer up approved lives that are acceptable to God through Jesus Christ! When God chooses us (Matthew 22:14), He sets us apart and when we yield, we become even more precious to Him. Not everyone will agree with you when you choose to whole-heartedly live for Christ, and some will even reject you or try to persuade you to do otherwise.

I was speaking with a close minister friend of mine one day, and he shared some much-appreciated wisdom with me. He said something like, "We can't worry about the things we have no control over; God is in control – He's got it – we just have to stay in a place of thanksgiving." First Thessalonians 5:18 says, *"In everything give thanks; for this is the will of God in Christ Jesus for you."*

Just taste and see that the Lord our God is good and that as we drink from His eternal-life-giving Word, stay in a place of thanksgiving – no matter what obstacle comes your way. God's got it! Hallelujah!

In everything give thanks; for this is the will of God
in Christ Jesus for you (1 Thessalonians 5:18).

Divine Punch

Recipe

Divine Punch

Ingredients:
    Two 2 liter bottles ginger ale
    2 packages frozen fruit punch concentrate
    2 packages frozen pineapple concentrate

Directions:

1. In a large punch bowl, mix your ginger ale, frozen fruit punch, and frozen pineapple juice together until everything is melted and mixed. Serves 12 or more, depending on the size of the cups.

Serves 12 or more

Nutrition Facts

Calories	405.9	Vitamin A	0.0 %
		Vitamin B-12	0.0 %
Total Fat 0.0 g		Vitamin B-6	0.0 %
Saturated Fat	0.0 g	Vitamin C	220.0 %
Polyunsaturated Fat	0.0 g	Vitamin D	0.0 %
Monounsaturated Fat	0.0 g	Vitamin E	0.0 %
Cholesterol	0.0 mg	Calcium	1.5 %
Sodium	59.2 mg	Copper	4.4 %
Potassium	264.9 mg	Folate	0.0 %
Total Carbohydrate	105.8 g	Iron	4.9 %
Dietary Fiber	0.0 g	Magnesium	1.2 %
Sugars	99.5 g	Manganese	3.2 %
Protein	1.1 g	Niacin	0.0 %
		Pantothenic Acid	0.0 %
		Phosphorus	0.0 %
		Riboflavin	0.0 %
		Selenium	0.7 %
		Thiamin	0.0 %
		Zinc	1.6 %

And it is a good thing to receive wealth from God and the good health to enjoy it. To enjoy your work and accept your lot in life – this is indeed a gift from God (Ecclesiastes 5:19 NLT).

Spring Soul Food

In Good Hands

Ecclesiastes 5:8 - 20 (NLT) says,

Don't be surprised if you see a poor person being oppressed by the powerful and if justice is being miscarried throughout the land. For every official is under orders from higher up, and matters of justice get lost in red tape and bureaucracy. Even the king milks the land for his own profit! Those who love money will never have enough. How meaningless to think that wealth brings true happiness! The more you have, the more people come to help you spend it. So what good is wealth — except perhaps to watch it slip through your fingers! People who work hard sleep well, whether they eat little or much. But the rich seldom get a good night's sleep. There is another serious problem I have seen under the sun. Hoarding riches harms the saver. Money is put into risky investments that turn sour, and everything is lost. In the end, there is nothing left to pass on to one's children. We all come to the end of our lives as naked and empty-handed as on the day we were born. We can't take our riches with us. And this, too, is a very serious problem. People leave this world no better off than when they came. All their hard work is for nothing – like working for the wind. Throughout their lives, they live under a cloud–frustrated discouraged, and angry. Even so, I have noticed one thing, at least, that is good. It is good for people to eat, drink, and enjoy their work under the sun during the short life God has given them, and to accept their lot in life. And it is a good thing to receive wealth from God and the good health to enjoy it. To enjoy your work and accept your lot in life – this is indeed a gift from God. God keeps such people so busy enjoying life that they take no time to brood over the past.

In recent times, we've witnessed an awful array of economic turmoil, frustration, greed, ignorance, exclusion, mishandling, deception, loss, and discord – none of which are good. According to the Word of God (Ecclesiastes 5:8), we should not be surprised that these things are happening. Galatians 6:7 says, *"Do not be deceived, God is not mocked; for whatever a man sows, that he will also reap."* The ungodly seeds (war, deceit, stealing, murder, lying, etc.) sown by the governing body of our country (as well as the generational wealthy families that have run this country) have come to a head. The very foundation of the United States was built by the hard labor of African slaves and natives. Much of the land was acquired by settlers deceiving and murdering the natives. The financial structure of this land was deceptively and exclusively devised for the 5%

who are wealthy. This country's love of money is the root of all kinds evil that has been perpetuated since before its incorporation. First Timothy 6:10 reads, *"For the love of money is a root of all kinds of evil, for which some have strayed from the faith in their greediness, and pierced themselves through with many sorrows.*

Many people do not recognize the fact that we all come to the end of our lives as naked and empty-handed as on the day we were born (Ecclesiastes 5:15). This is one of the reasons why we, the followers of Jesus Christ, store up eternal treasures in heaven with our adherence to the commandments of God here on earth. Remember, if we desire for our children to be blessed and not cursed, let us sow good seeds so that our children's inheritance is blessed.

In the midst of the uproar that's going on around us, the Word of God says we are to be content with our lot in life. As we continue to sow good seeds and work hard, our lots will change; our abundance will change; our levels of prosperity will change; and in each season, whether it's a season of lack or abundance, let us be content. Be careful not to allow the frustrations, anger, and discouragements of our past or current situations bombard us, because they can and will affect our health. We want to thoroughly enjoy the reparations that are coming to us, so let us stay in a place of joy and thanksgiving as we accept our present lot. *"And it is a good thing to receive wealth from God and the good health to enjoy it. To enjoy your work and accept your lot in life—this is indeed a gift from God"* (Ecclesiastes 5:19 NLT).

Despite all that's going on, I have good news! God has shown up on behalf of His people, you and me! Reparations are on the way! Don't fret over the misfortunes of the economy. No matter how bad the matters around us get, our economy is in good hands with Jesus!

Do not be deceived, God is not mocked; for whatever a man sows, that he will also reap (Galatians 6:7).

Heavenly Chicken Salad
Finger Sandwiches

Recipe

Heavenly Chicken Salad Finger Sandwiches

Ingredients:
4 small cans chunk chicken in water
2 small cans crushed pineapple
1 small bag chopped pecans
1 package fresh celery
1 large container Miracle Whip
1 - 3 loaves of bread (of your choice)

Directions:

1. First, using a bread knife, slice the crust off of your bread slices.

2. Next, chop your celery (enough for 1 full cup).

3. In a large bowl, combine your 4 small cans of chunk chicken (drained), 2 small cans of crushed pineapple with juice, 1 full cup of chopped pecans, 1 full cup of chopped celery, and 1full cup of miracle whip.

4. Mix ingredients very well.

5. Spread as much or as little on your bread slices as you'd like, then cut the sandwiches into 4 squares or triangles.

Serves 20 or more

Nutrition Facts

Calories	441.5	Vitamin A	0.0 %
Total Fat	24.8 g	Vitamin B-12	0.0 %
Saturated Fat	2.2 g	Vitamin B-6	1.1 %
Polyunsaturated Fat	1.8 g	Vitamin C	20.0 %
Monounsaturated Fat	0.2 g	Vitamin D	0.0 %
Cholesterol	25.0 mg	Vitamin E	0.5 %
Sodium	450.3 mg	Calcium	5.8 %
Potassium	175.0 mg	Copper	3.2 %
Total Carbohydrate	36.7 g	Folate	6.9 %
Dietary Fiber	4.6 g	Iron	11.2 %
Sugars	19.1 g	Magnesium	1.4 %
Protein	20.9 g	Manganese	6.0 %
		Niacin	5.5 %
		Pantothenic Acid	0.5 %
		Phosphorus	2.5 %
		Riboflavin	4.9 %
		Selenium	6.2 %
		Thiamin	7.6 %
		Zinc	1.2 %

If any of you lacks wisdom, let him ask God, who gives to all generously and without reproach, and it will be given to him (James 1:5).

Spring
Soul Food

Nonselective Wisdom

First Timothy 4:12 - 16 reads,

Let no one despise your youth, but be an example to the believers in word, in conduct, in love, in spirit, in faith, in purity. Till I come, give attention to reading, to exhortation, to doctrine. Do not neglect the gift that is in you, which was given to you by prophecy with the laying on of the hands of the eldership. Meditate on these things; give yourself entirely to them, that your progress may be evident to all. Take heed to yourself and to the doctrine. Continue in them, for in doing this you will save both yourself and those who hear you.

Being the youngest in your family, group of friends, or group of co-workers can have both benefits and drawbacks. Many times people believe that wisdom only comes from experience...that it's something you acquire only with age. It's true that wisdom does come from experience, but experience is not the only source – or even the best source – of wisdom. Yes, our elders should have wisdom to share with those of us who are younger, but they shouldn't be so quick to discredit the wisdom of younger folks. God is more than able to pour out His wisdom upon all willing vessels, which includes the young.

I am often-times amazed at the God-given wisdom of my wife. I've bared witness on several occasions to the in-depth spiritual insight she expresses in so many of life's seasons. Most of the time, her wisdom comes not from experience but from Christ. It doesn't take going through the same trials as those who have gone before us to gain wisdom and knowledge. The one and only true wisdom is Godly wisdom. Too often worldly knowledge is confused with Godly wisdom and, in turn, passed on as such. We must accurately discern the difference between the two! What we have learned from the world is worldly knowledge, not Godly wisdom! This traditional way of thinking is and has been a stumbling block to the unlimited power of God working in us. For this reason alone, it is vitally important that we each seek first the kingdom of God (Matthew 6:33) for ourselves!

> *For to one is given the word of wisdom through the Spirit, and to another the word of knowledge according to the same Spirit; to another faith by the same Spirit, and to another gifts of healing by the one Spirit, and to another the effecting of miracles, and to another prophecy, and to another the distinguishing of spirits, to another various kinds of tongues, and to another the interpretation of tongues. But one and the same Spirit works all these*

things, distributing to each one individually just as He wills (1 Corinthians 12:8 11 NASB).

Wisdom from God our Father in heaven is nonselective when it comes to age so much so that He chose an eight-year-old to be king. Second Kings 22:1 reads, *"Josiah was eight years old when he became king, and he reigned thirty-one years in Jerusalem; and his mother's name was Jedidah the daughter of Adaiah of Bozkath."* God can use anyone he deems fit for the job. Whether you're young or old, remember that James 1:5 says, *"If any of you lacks wisdom, let him ask God, who gives to all generously and without reproach, and it will be given to him."*

Wisdom comes from listening (Proverbs 1:23 - 28), wisdom comes from reading the Word of God (Psalm 119: 91 - 104), wisdom is not limited by age (2 Chronicles 34:3), and most importantly, we should always ask God for wisdom (1 Kings 3:6 - 9). He's the best source, He's gives it freely, and His wisdom is nonselective!

May glory be unto the Lord our God forever! Amen!

Three Cheese Macaroni & Cheese

Recipe

Three Cheese Macaroni & Cheese

Ingredients:

4 cups uncooked elbow macaroni
6 tablespoons butter (or margarine)
2 eggs (beaten)
½ teaspoon salt
½ teaspoon pepper
3 cups milk
2 cups shredded mild cheddar cheese
2 cups shredded mozzarella cheese
2 cups shredded sharp cheddar cheese

Directions:

1. Cook your elbow macaroni until done according to the directions on the box.
2. Drain the macaroni in a strainer.
3. In a casserole dish, mix the macaroni, butter, salt, pepper, milk, mozzarella, sharp cheddar, and 1 cup of the mild cheddar cheese.
4. Stir in the eggs.
5. Cover the mixture with aluminum foil and bake it for 45 minutes at 350 degrees Fahrenheit.
6. After 45 minutes, uncover the dish and add 1 cup of mild cheddar cheese to the top of the macaroni. Then bake the dish uncovered for 10 more minutes.

Serves 8 or more

Nutrition Facts

Calories	629.0
Total Fat	27.7 g
Saturated Fat	15.5 g
Polyunsaturated Fat	2.3 g
Monounsaturated Fat	2.5 g
Cholesterol	79.5 mg
Sodium	3,117.2 mg
Potassium	28.7 mg
Total Carbohydrate	58.9 g
Dietary Fiber	2.6 g
Sugars	13.4 g
Protein	37.4 g

Vitamin A	24.7 %
Vitamin B-12	0.1 %
Vitamin B-6	0.4 %
Vitamin C	1.6 %
Vitamin D	0.0 %
Vitamin E	0.1 %
Calcium	69.7 %
Copper	1.3 %
Folate	0.1 %
Iron	3.9 %
Magnesium	1.1 %
Manganese	6.2 %
Niacin	0.1 %
Pantothenic Acid	0.0 %
Phosphorus	0.5 %
Riboflavin	0.4 %
Selenium	0.1 %
Thiamin	0.2 %
Zinc	0.2 %

Give therefore thy servant an understanding heart to judge thy people, that I may discern between good and bad: for who is able to judge this thy so great a people?
(1Kings 3:9)

I say then: Walk in the Spirit, and you shall not fulfill the lust of the flesh (Galatians 5:16).

Summer Soul Food

We Think We Have It All Figured Out

In this journey called life, we like to be prepared for the unexpected. It's not a pleasant feeling to be caught off guard by unpredictable "seasons." To circumvent undesired situations, we try to prepare by saving money for unexpected financial burdens and stocking up on necessities just in case the need arises. It gives us a sense of comfort to have a mental solution to all the "what if" questions we conjure up. But in many cases we find ourselves ill prepared, not having enough to satisfy the solution to the circumstance. At least that's what some of us think. Let's examine some of what the Word of God says about our way of thinking.

> For My thoughts are not your thoughts, nor are your ways My ways," says the Lord. "For as the heavens are higher than the earth, so are My ways higher than your ways, and My thoughts than your thoughts. For as the rain comes down, and the snow from heaven, and do not return there, but water the earth, and make it bring forth and bud, that it may give seed to the sower and bread to the eater, so shall My word be that goes forth from My mouth; it

shall not return to Me void, but it shall accomplish
what I please, and it shall prosper in the thing for
which I sent it (Isaiah 55:8).

Many of us like to think we have it all figured
out. Whether it's our plan for school, our career, our
family, the next day, or our children, we like to have
some idea of where we're going and how we're going
to get there. It's nice to have that comfort, but if what
we plan for ourselves is not in line and in agreement
with what God has for us, He has His way of taking us
out of our comfort zone and increasing our flexibility to
accomplish what He desires for us.

So, how do we increase our flexibility to accomplish
what God desires for us? One answer is found in Romans
12:1. The Apostle Paul writes, *"I beseech you therefore,
brethren, by the mercies of God, that you present your
bodies a living sacrifice, holy, acceptable unto God,
which is your reasonable service."* By presenting our
bodies as living sacrifices that are holy and acceptable
to God, we are saying, "Lord, I yield to Your will for my
life." We are saying, "Not my will, God, but Your will be
done in my life."

When we yield, we enter into His spiritual current.
Like a river current, if you fight against it, you will wear
yourself down to the point of exhaustion and possible
drowning. But if you go with the flow of the current,
it will take you to the destination it has for you! You
had to read that last statement with your spiritual eyes.

Unlike a natural river current, the spiritual current of God our Father keeps us in perfect peace, strengthens us with His joy, provides all of our needs, gives us the victory in Jesus' name, prepares a table before us in the presence of our enemies, never leaves us nor forsakes us, gives us life and that more abundantly, and is with us even until the end of the age! (Just to name a few.)

It's a sacrifice on our part to yield to the "spiritual current" of God. When we sacrifice something – whether it's time, money, our home, or possessions – we willingly (or sometimes, unwillingly) give up custody of it. To present our bodies as living sacrifices means giving up custody of our flesh and placing ourselves under the subjection of the Holy Spirit. We accomplish this by putting our flesh "to death" through feeding our spirit the infallible Word of God.

One might ask, "What about peer pressure and the things that my flesh struggles with day in and day out?" (for example, alcohol, smoking, drugs, pornography, cursing, sexual immorality, malice, deceit, gossiping, lying, etc.). Here's how we combat these things that we war against every day: Galatians 5:16 reads, *"I say then: Walk in the Spirit, and you shall not fulfill the lust of the flesh."* In order to walk in the Spirit we must continuously seek God's Word and nurture that part of us that longs for Him. By doing so, we grow in our wisdom and understanding, we become spiritually stronger and aware, and we recognize what's fleshly vs. what's spirit; for we do not wrestle against flesh and blood but against principalities, against powers, against the rulers of the darkness of this age, and against spiritual hosts of wickedness in heavenly places (Ephesians 6:12).

When we completely yield to the will of God, we enter a whole new dimension of abundant life and prosperous living. More importantly, we're in the will of God, and He will never leave you hanging.

For we wrestle not against flesh and blood, but against principalities, against powers, against the rulers of the darkness of this world, against spiritual wickedness in high [places] (Ephesians 6:12).

Stand Alone Grilled Chicken

Recipe

Stand Alone Grilled Chicken

Ingredints:
1 (10 pound) bag of chicken leg quarters
lemon pepper seasoning
seasoned salt
apple cider vinegar

You'll Need:
1. Large Zip Lock storage bags
2. Kingsford charcoal (or your preference)
3. lighter fluid
4. one large aluminum pan for seasoning
5. one large aluminum pan for removal from grill
6. a grill (a standard home grill is fine)
7. food handling gloves (clear polyethylene)
8. barbeque sauce (optional)

Directions:

Day 1

1. The day or night before you actually cook, remove and discard the skin from the chicken leg quarters.

NOTE: Because you will be handling raw poultry and for health safety reasons, be sure hot water and soap are immediately available after handling the meat for cleaning. Make sure that you isolate the area from any other food or items so that you don't cross contaminate. One last thing: PLEASE be sure to thoroughly clean the area with disinfectant and soap and water after you finish preparing the chicken (this includes your hands).

2. After removing the skin from the leg quarters, evenly season and cover every side of the chicken with seasoned salt, lemon pepper, and garlic powder. Be sure not to over season.
3. Place the seasoned chicken in large Zip Lock storage bags, then place the Zip Lock bags in the large aluminum pan. Place the aluminum pan in the refrigerator overnight (separate from other refrigerated products).

33

Day 2

4.   Make sure you scrub and clean your grill using a grill scrub brush, hot water, and mild soap. Rinse the grill thoroughly after cleaning. Place the charcoal evenly on the base of the grill, lightly soak the charcoal with lighter fluid, and ignite.

NOTE: Exercise extreme caution when dealing with fire and fuel. Allow all the charcoal to gray over. Make sure your grill vents are open. Now you are ready to begin ...

5.   Place chicken on the grill. Once you have placed the amount of chicken the grill can safely handle, close the hood and allow the chicken to cook 10 - 15 minutes before turning.
6.   Turn repeat on the other side. At this time, take your apple cider vinegar and lightly sprinkle it directly on the side of the chicken that is facing up.
7.   Allow the chicken to cook another 10 - 15 minutes before turning.
8.   Repeat on the other side. Flip one more time and allow both sides to cook 15 more minutes on each side. The inside temperature of the center of your grilled chicken should be at least 150 degrees Fahrenheit. At this temperature, your chicken is ready.

Serves 8 or more.

Nutrition Facts

Calories	154. 3		Vitamin A	0.0 %
Total Fat	8.0 g		Vitamin B-12	0.0 %
Saturated Fat	2.0 g		Vitamin B-6	4.1 %
Polyunsaturated Fat	0.0 g		Vitamin C	0.8 %
Monounsaturated Fat	0.0 g		Vitamin D	0.0 %
Cholesterol	44.0 mg		Vitamin E	0.0 %
Sodium	770.7 mg		Calcium	0.2 %
Potassium	30.8 mg		Copper	0.2 %
Total Carbohydrate	2.0 g		Folate	0.0 %
Dietary Fiber	0.3 g		Iron	0.4 %
Sugars	0.7 g		Magnesium	0.4 %
Protein	18.5 g		Manganese	0.8 %
			Niacin	0.1 %
			Pantothenic Acid	0.0 %
			Phosphorus	1.2 %
			Riboflavin	0.3 %
			Selenium	1.5 %
			Thiamin	0.9 %
			Zinc	0.5 %

35

Therefore by Him let us continually offer the sacrifice of praise to God, that is, the fruit of our lips, giving thanks to His name. But do not forget to do good and to share, for with such sacrifices God is well pleased (Hebrews 13:15 - 16).

Summer Soul Food

What to Do in Expectation of New Things

It is my hope and prayer that this word finds you in expectation of a miraculous release of new things. For some it's monetary increase, for some new found health, for some new relationships, for some forgiven debts, for some natural conception and birth, for some new ministry, or all the above and much more.

As we anticipate the blessings of God, let us remember *Hebrews 13:15 - 16, "Therefore by Him let us continually offer the sacrifice of praise to God, that is, the fruit of our lips, giving thanks to His name. But do not forget to do good and to share, for with such sacrifices God is well pleased."* A fruit-bearing tree cannot bear fruit unless it receives proper nourishment from the soil in which it's planted, but this can only happen if the soil is fertile. Water and essential minerals must be frequently added to the soil in order to maintain a preferable environment for optimal growth and fruit production or occurrences such as construction, drought, and biological breakdown will strip the soil of its essential substance and in turn cause no fruit to grow.

The same can be said concerning our spiritual soil. You might ask, "How do we fertilize our spiritual soil so that we will bear the good fruit of praise from our lips and please God?" Jesus says it best in John 7:37–38: *"If anyone thirsts, let him come to Me and drink. He who believes in Me, as the Scripture has said, out of his heart will flow rivers of living water."* Luke 6:45 says, *"...For out of the abundance of the heart his mouth speaks."* If we "drink" the Word of God, we are provided everything we need to fertilize our ground so that we bear the fruit of praise from our lips to God.

Let us also not forget to do good to others and to share our blessings. And as we share, remember that Hebrews 13:1-2 says, *"Let brotherly love continue. Do not forget to entertain strangers, for by so doing some have unwittingly entertained angels."* Especially because of the time in which we live, allow the Holy Spirit to guide you in your discerning of spirits before you entertain. Amen!

If anyone thirsts, let him come to Me and drink. He who believes in Me, as the Scripture has said, out of his heart will flow rivers of living water (John 7:37–38).

Divine Potato Salad

Recipe

Divine Potato Salad

Ingredients:

6 large baking potatoes (any brand works)
3 eggs
½ teaspoon of salt
2/3 cup of miracle whip
5 ounces of sweet relish
paprika for a finishing touch

Directions:

1. First, boil your potatoes on medium-high heat until done. Be sure not overcook (a fork should penetrate the potatoes with slight resistance).
2. Once the potatoes are done, remove them from the heat and place them in cold water to cool.
3. Boil your eggs on medium-high heat until hard-boiled.
4. Once the eggs are done, remove them from the heat and place them in cold water to cool.
5. Once the potatoes are cool enough for handling, peel the potatoes and slice them into chunks (approximately 1 inch by 1 inch)
6. Peel and slice the eggs into small pieces (approximately ½ inch cubes)
7. Stir all ingredients in gently (except paprika).
8. Once all ingredients are well mixed, spoon the mixture into a bowl.
9. Add paprika lightly across the top.
10. Store the salad in the refrigerator until ready to be served.

Serves 8 or more

Nutrition Facts

Amount Per Servings	
Calories 213.9	
Total Fat 8.0 g	
Saturated Fat 2.2 g	
Polyunsaturated Fat 2.8 g	
Monounsaturated Fat 2.0 g	
Cholesterol 213.0 mg	
Sodium 2,507.8 mg	
Potassium 882.2 mg	
Total Carbohydrate 33.1 g	
Dietary Fiber 5.6 g	
Sugars 4.7 g	
Protein 7.8 g	

Vitamin A	77.1 %
Vitamin B-12	3.7 %
Vitamin B-6	26.0 %
Vitamin C	53.2 %
Vitamin D	0.0 %
Vitamin E	4.5 %
Calcium	3.4 %
Copper	6.2 %
Folate	12.9 %
Iron	17.6 %
Magnesium	9.2 %
Manganese	3.2 %
Niacin	13.3 %
Pantothenic Acid	1.2 %
Phosphorus	2.4 %
Riboflavin	15.5 %
Selenium	0.4 %
Thiamin	11.0 %
Zinc	6.7 %

*Let brotherly love continue. Do not forget to entertain
strangers, for by so doing some have unwittingly
entertained angels (Hebrews 13:1 - 2).*

Either make the tree good and its fruit good, or else make the tree bad and its fruit bad; for a tree is known by its fruit (Matthew 12:33).

Summer Soul Food

Are You Bearing Good Fruit

In Matthew 12:33, Jesus says, *"Either make the tree good and its fruit good, or else make the tree bad and its fruit bad; for a tree is known by its fruit."* After meditating on the Word and seeking God's guidance for what it is He would have me feed His people, a question came to mind: what kind of fruit are you known to bear?

Are you known to bear the works of the flesh (a.k.a. bad fruit)? The people of Galatians 5:19 - 21 sure are. They are guilty of adultery, fornication, uncleanness, lewdness (unlawful sexual intercourse or disregarding sexual restraints), idolatry, sorcery (witchcraft), hatred, contentions (rivalry), jealousies, outbursts of wrath, selfish ambitions, dissensions (quarrelling), heresies (an opinion or practice contrary to the truth), envy, murders, drunkenness, revelries (noisy partying), and the like of which will cause those who practice them not to inherit the kingdom of God. Or, are you known to bear the fruit of the Spirit (love, joy, peace, longsuffering, kindness, goodness, faithfulness, gentleness, and self-control), as the people of Galatians 5:22 – 23 are?

If we allow our flesh to control our actions, trouble follows, laws are broken, people are offended, families are torn, diseases are spread, and sickness manifests. But if we allow the fruit of the Spirit to govern us, there is no law against us. What trouble or broken laws can be had from love, joy, peace, longsuffering, kindness, goodness, faithfulness, gentleness, and self-control? According to the Word of God, none!

Tomorrow is not promised. So when we exit out of one day and into a brand new day, we are witnessing the love of God manifested because of His grace and mercy! We are given another opportunity to bear good fruit! Grace is the unmerited favor we receive solely because God loves us with a love that surpasses all understanding. Mercy is God's compassion towards us. God's grace and mercy can be summarized as undeserved favor and kindness. As we experience the manifested love of God, ask yourself, *"What kind of fruit am I known to bear?"* for *"a tree is known by its fruit"* (Matthew 12:33).

Good fruit comes from a good seed. The good seed is the Word of God! *"But You, O Lord, are a God full of compassion, and gracious, longsuffering and abundant in mercy and truth"* (Psalm 86:15). *"The earth, O Lord, is full of Your mercy; teach me Your statutes*" (Psalm 119:64).

Praise the Lord for His mercy endures forever!

Summer Pie

Recipe

Summer Pie

Ingredients:
½ cup lemon juice
1 cup chopped nuts
1 can Eagle brand condensed milk
2 small cans mandarin oranges (drained)
1 large (12 oz) container cool whip
1 small can crushed pineapple
2 gram cracker pie shells

Directions:
1. Mix the lemon juice and milk in a large bowl.
2. Fold in the cool whip
3. Add the nuts, oranges, and pineapple
4. Pour the mixture into the pie shells
5. Refrigerate until firm.

Serves 8. Enjoy!

Nutrition Facts

Amount Per 8 Servings			Vitamin A	0.5 %
Calories 735.5			Vitamin B-12	0.0 %
Total Fat 16.0 g			Vitamin B-6	3.1 %
Saturated Fat	3.0 g		Vitamin C	113.5 %
Polyunsaturated Fat		2.5 g	Vitamin D	0.0 %
Monounsaturated Fat		4.5 g	Vitamin E	0.5 %
Cholesterol	0.0 mg		Calcium	0.9 %
Sodium 161.2 mg			Copper	1.8 %
Potassium	736.3 mg		Folate	4.0 %
Total Carbohydrate		138.0 g	Iron	6.2 %
Dietary Fiber	18.9 g		Magnesium	1.8 %
Sugars	117.4 g		Manganese	0.5 %
Protein 8.5 g			Niacin	0.6 %
			Pantothenic Acid	1.3 %
			Phosphorus	0.7 %
			Riboflavin	0.7 %
			Selenium	0.2 %
			Thiamin	2.4 %
			Zinc	0.4 %

What then shall we say to these things? If God is for us, who can be against us? (Romans 8:31).

Fall
Soul Food

A Cerebral Battle

The battlefield of the mind is an intricate part of our spiritual walk. As we grow spiritually, we learn to decipher with precision between our own, God's, and the enemy's voice. But prior to reaching such a level, we battle constant attempts by the devil to cause the type of confusion that can seriously plague us mentally. These things are known as distractions. We must be careful and spiritually aware of the source and timing of these distractions. They usually come during times of spiritual growth, maturity, and divine release. When we are in line with God and His plans for our lives (*seeking first the kingdom of God and His righteousness,* as stated in Matthew 6:33), the enemy will try everything to knock us off course! The enemy will use anyone or anything he can especially those closest to your heart —to try to manipulate and control you, cause you to doubt, provoke you, or even steal what's yours! "*What then shall we say to these things? If God is for us, who can be against us?"* (Romans 8:31).

I was strengthened by something my wife said one time while I was just casually talking with her. She said (and I'm paraphrasing), "When distractions come, we must change our response; instead of giving in to the distractions and saying things like, 'Here we go again,' 'Why, Lord, why,' or 'I'm sick of this mess,' we should be saying and believing that 'God is doing something!' Ephesians 6:12 reads, *"For we do not wrestle against flesh and blood, but against principalities, against powers, against the rulers of the darkness of this age, against spiritual hosts of wickedness in the heavenly places."* Therefore, submit to God. Resist the devil and he will flee from you (James 4:7)! The enemy only has power over us if we let him have it! We have the victory in Jesus' name!

We must not be stagnant in our relationship with God. In other words, do not be content with where you are in your walk and relationship with Jesus just because it's comfortable and easy for you. We must continually seek God and what it is He would have us to do. We must come out of our spiritual comfort zone and acquire a desire to grow in Christ Jesus! Jesus says in Matthew 6:10, *"Your kingdom come. Your will be done, on earth as it is in heaven."* God's will is being done and will continue to be done, so we might as well get on board!

As we grow in Christ, God requires more of us. That means more of our time in prayer, praise and worship, communication with Him, talking with Him, reading His Word, and seeking Him first in all things (relationships, family matters, work, school, business, all decisions, etc.).

When we are blessed to see tomorrow become today, we are witnessing God's infinite love for us! Are we expressing our sincere gratitude, love, and appreciation in spirit and in truth to God with praise and worship? John 4:23 says, *"But the hour is coming, and now is, when the true worshipers will worship the Father in spirit and truth; for the Father is seeking such to worship Him."* We cannot worship God in spirit and in truth if we are harboring things in our hearts that manifest as complaining, ill feelings toward one another, gossiping about and slandering one another, and spreading rumors and untruths about one another. When the Word of God rules, abides, and is hidden in our hearts, there is no room for negative actions! *"Your word I have hidden in my heart, that I might not sin against You"* (Psalm 119:11). Remember that Jesus says in Matthew 7:12, *"Therefore, whatever you want men to do to you, do also to them, for this is the Law and the Prophets."*

Continue to seek God in all things, and His blessings will blow your mind! Don't be distracted and miss what God is doing. Be in expectation of signs, wonders, and miracles. Remember Joshua 1:9: *"Have I not commanded you? Be strong and of good courage; do not be afraid, nor dismayed, for the Lord God is with you wherever you go."*

Have I not commanded you? Be strong and of good courage; do not be afraid, nor dismayed, for the Lord God is with you wherever you go (Joshua 1:9).

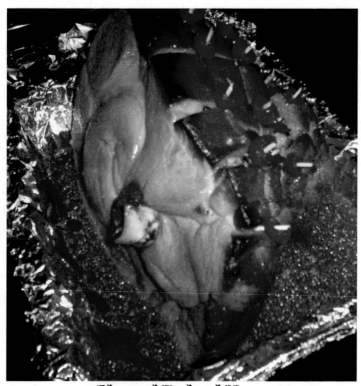

Glazed Baked Ham

Recipe

Glazed Baked Ham

Ingredients:
1 (10 - 12 lb) whole ham
1 cup pancake maple syrup
2 cups brown sugar
one 20-ounce can of crushed pineapple
whole cloves
1 tablespoon cornstarch
maraschino cherries cut in half
large aluminum or roasting pan
aluminum foil

1. Remove the ham from the plastic wrap and rinse it thoroughly.
2. Cut any excess fat from the ham, but leave some for flavor.
3. Score the ham with a sharp knife into 1 inch by 1 inch squares deep enough to hold the whole cloves. Insert desired amount of whole cloves.
4. Preheat your oven to 350 degrees Fahrenheit.
5. While the oven is preheating, take this time to mix your brown sugar and maple syrup for basting.
6. Mix 2 cups of brown sugar with the 1 cup of pancake maple syrup.
7. Place the mixture to the side until ready for use.
8. Cover the ham with aluminum foil, leaving some space between the foil and ham.
9. Place the ham in the oven for 1 hour on the bottom oven rack.
10. While the ham is cooking, mix your crushed pineapple (with juice), 1 tablespoon of cornstarch, 2 table spoons of syrup, and the brown sugar mixture in a saucepan. Heat the mixture to a boil, stirring frequently, until the sauce thickens.

11. Remove from heat.

12. After it has been in the oven for 1 hour, remove the foil and baste the ham with the maple syrup and brown sugar mixture (a cake spatula works well to spread the mixture).

13. Place the ham back into the oven (uncovered) for another 30 minutes, then repeat the basting step.

14. Repeat this step over the next hour and a half every 30 minutes. Be sure that the center of the ham has reached at least 150 degrees Fahrenheit before removing it from the oven.

15. The total cook time for your ham should be 3 to 3.5 hours.

16. Your ham is ready to be sliced and served when the center temperature has reached 150 degrees.

NOTE: Because you will be handling pork and for health safety reasons, be sure hot water and soap are immediately available after handling the meat for cleaning. Make sure that you isolate the area from any other food so that you don't cross contaminate. Finally, PLEASE be sure to thoroughly clean the area with disinfectant and soap and warm water after you finish preparing the ham (this includes your hands).

Serves 10 or more.

Nutrition Facts

Calories	157.94		Vitamin A	0.7 %
Total Fat	1.0 g		Vitamin B-12	0.0 %
Saturated Fat	3.0 g		Vitamin B-6	2.3 %
Polyunsaturated Fat	0.8 g		Vitamin C	28.9 %
Monounsaturated Fat	0.3 g		Vitamin D	0.0 %
Cholesterol	55.0 mg		Vitamin E	0.6 %
Sodium	124.6 mg		Calcium	25.9 %
Potassium	85.0 mg		Copper	16.4 %
Total Carbohydrate	35.3 g		Folate	1.5 %
Dietary Fiber	.4 g		Iron	29.6 %
Sugars	20.5 g		Magnesium	16.4 %
Protein	1.8 g		Manganese	622.0 %
			Niacin	1.0 %
			Pantothenic Acid	1.2 %
			Phosphorus	3.0 %
			Riboflavin	2.9 %
			Selenium	8.4 %
			Thiamin	1.8 %
			Zinc	88.4 %

59

Out of the same mouth proceed blessing and cursing.
My brethren, these things ought not to be so
(James 3:10).

Fall Soul Food

You Are What You Speak

Proverbs 18:21 says, *"Death and life are in the power of the tongue, and those who love it will eat its fruit."* Every day, whether on the news, in the workplace, amongst our families, amongst our friends, or even in the church, we hear words of all kinds uttered from the mouths of our brothers, sisters, friends, family members, colleagues, and even ourselves. Sometimes they're blessings, sometimes they're curses, and sometimes they're both. *"Out of the same mouth proceed blessing and cursing. My brethren, these things ought not to be so"* (James 3:10). Day in and day out we're speaking things into our own lives, our children's lives, and any other life we encounter. We must be cautious and cognizant of what we speak. Jesus says in Matthew 15:11, *"Not what goes into the mouth defiles a man; but what comes out of the mouth, this defiles a man."*

61

As it pertains to our children, we oftentimes unconsciously speak negative things concerning them. We say things like, "I can't do anything with them" or "that child is greedy" or "that child is selfish" or "that child is lazy." If you stop and think for just a moment about how your children are behaving and remember the words you've spoken concerning them, hopefully you will realize that your words are shaping your child's life, behavior, and character. There is power in the tongue!

Instead of cursing our children, we ought to be blessing our children. The overall state of our present-day youth speaks volumes of how desperately a change for the better is needed! We should say positive and encouraging things like, "he is a good kid," or "she is smart," or "he is a blessing!" Yes, saying these things may very well be the total opposite of the truth, but remember Jesus' words in Matthew 11:12: *"And from the days of John the Baptist until now the kingdom of heaven suffers violence, and the violent take it by force."* Forcefully speak the good things into your children and bind the negative things. Bind those negative things in the only name that has power – Jesus Christ! Bind bad behavior in Jesus' name! Bind laziness in Jesus' name! Bind meanness in Jesus' name! Jesus says in Matthew 18:18, *"Assuredly, I say to you, whatever you bind on earth will be bound in heaven, and whatever you loose on earth will be loosed in heaven."* Loose good behavior! Loose the Holy Spirit! Loose unselfishness! Loose politeness! Loose humbleness! Loose obedience! Loose healing! Loose integrity! How do you bind and loose these things? You bind and loosen them by speaking them from your mouth. There is power in the tongue!

Not only should we be cautious and cognizant of what we speak into the lives of those around us, but we must also be cautious and cognizant of what we speak into our own lives. We often say negative things like these concerning ourselves: "I'm broke," "I'm lazy," "I'm stubborn," "I'm stressed," or "I'm depressed." Again, if you stop and think for just a moment about your situation and how you are behaving and remember the words you've spoken about yourself, hopefully you will realize that your words are shaping your life, behavior, and character. Speak positive things into your life: "I am not broken," "I am smart," "I am a child of the true and living God," "I am who God says I am," "I am prosperous," "I am not depressed," "I am not crazy," "I am healed," "I am victorious!" There is power in the tongue!

Romans 4:16 - 18 says,

Therefore it is of faith that it might be according to grace, so that the promise might be sure to all the seed, not only to those who are of the law, but also to those who are of the faith of Abraham, who is the father of us all (as it is written, "I have made you

*a father of many nations") in the presence of Him
whom he believed – God, who gives life to the dead
and calls those things which do not exist as though
they did; who, contrary to hope, in hope believed,
so that he became the father of many nations, according to what was spoken, "So shall your descen-
dants be."*

Speak those good things that are not as though they were not only for yourself, but also for your children, and any other lives you impact and watch the power that God gives us in what we speak manifest! There is power in the tongue!!!!

We have often heard the phrase "you are what you eat" as it relates to the nutritional value of the choice of food we consume and how it affects our health. As it pertains to the choice of words we speak that shape our lives and character, you are what you speak!

*And from the days of John the Baptist until now the
kingdom of heaven suffers violence, and the violent
take it by force (Matthew 11:12).*

Soulful Collard Greens

Recipe

Soulful Collard Greens

Ingredients:
2 bags already cut collard green
1 package smoked turkey necks
3 tablespoons sugar
2/3 cup vegetable oil
2 tablespoons black pepper
2 tablespoons butter or margarine
2/3 cup apple cider vinegar

Directions:

1. Make sure you thoroughly wash your collard greens before cooking.
2. Fill a deep boiler half full with water and place it on the stove at medium-high heat.
3. Boil the turkey necks, butter, and black pepper.
4. Add the collard greens slowly.
5. Next, sprinkle the sugar evenly over the collard greens.
6. Now pour the vegetable oil and vinegar over the collard greens.
7. Cover the boiler and reduce the heat to low.
8. Cook for approximately 1.5 hours, checking the water level every 15 - 20 minutes.
9. Once the collard greens are tender, they are ready to serve.

Serves 8 or more.

Nutrition Facts

Calories	314.4	Vitamin A	8.4 %
Total Fat	29.6 g	Vitamin B-12	0.4 %
Saturated Fat	14.8 g	Vitamin B-6	2.1 %
Polyunsaturated Fat	1.8 g	Vitamin C	2.2 %
Monounsaturated Fat	4.7 g	Vitamin D	0.0 %
Cholesterol	36.3 mg	Vitamin E	10.6 %
Sodium	444.6 mg	Calcium	3.2 %
Potassium	95.6 mg	Copper	4.4 %
Total Carbohydrate	12.5 g	Folate	0.4 %
Dietary Fiber	3.2 g	Iron	11.5 %
Sugars	4.2 g	Magnesium	3.5 %
Protein	4.7 g	Manganese	18.1 %
		Niacin	1.2 %
		Pantothenic Acid	0.7 %
		Phosphorus	2.3 %
		Riboflavin	2.1 %
		Selenium	5.5 %
		Thiamin	0.7 %
		Zinc	5.4 %

Assuredly, I say to you, whatever you bind on earth will be bound in heaven, and whatever you loose on earth will be loosed in heaven (Matthew 18:18).

Be strong and of good courage, do not fear nor be afraid of them; for the Lord your God, He is the One who goes with you. He will not leave you nor forsake you (Deuteronomy 31:6).

Fall
Soul Food

Entering the New

Deuteronomy 31:6 says, *"Be strong and of good courage, do not fear nor be afraid of them; for the Lord your God, He is the One who goes with you. He will not leave you nor forsake you."* We are in the midst of a tremendous shift. Just as the children of Israel came to the bank of the Jordan River and Moses had reached the end of his journey, so are we the chosen people of God on the bank of our modern-day Jordan River, crossing into the Promised Land of our forefathers, and a new chosen leader has emerged! Moses knew that the new generation of Israelites needed encouragement. He knew they needed strengthening. The children of Israel needed to know that they could be courageous and strong, have what God says they can have, go where God says they can go, and be who God says they are!

For literally hundreds of years, the children of Israel had been use to the way things were. They were use to the bondage, they were use to the injustices, and they were use to the lack! This complacency with the status quo was passed down from generation to generation by word of mouth and, on an even deeper level, through DNA. Even though the new generation possessed this incapacitating tendency, they did not allow it to prevent them from inheriting the Promised Land. They chose to recognize the trap that such a mind-set had created for the previous generation. They remembered the forty years of wandering in the wilderness and seeing an entire generation die off because they were too afraid to go into the Promised Land and receive what God said He was going to give them.

Numbers 23:19 says, *"God is not a man, that He should lie, nor a son of man, that He should repent. Has He said, and will He not do? Or has He spoken, and will He not make it good?"* The new generation remembered that the lack of faith, the doubting, and the unbelief in what God said He would do for the previous generation snatched their inheritance from them and gave it to their children. After changing their mind-set and receiving the encouraging and strengthening words of their God-appointed leader, they walked into their promise, they inherited their promise, and they took back what was once theirs!

I was speaking with my brother on the phone one time, and he said something that strengthened me. We were talking about things going on in the work-place and he said something like, "We have to pray for the courage and strength to face and tactfully battle the injustices and potentially racially-motivated false persecutions that happen not only in the work-place, but also in the world." These types of happenings go deeper than what we see – there is a spiritual root. Ephesians 6:12 says, *"For we do not wrestle against flesh and blood, but against principalities, against powers, against the rulers of the darkness of this age, against spiritual hosts of wickedness in the heavenly places."* Remember the words of our Lord in Joshua 1:9 (*"Have I not commanded you? Be strong and of good courage; do not be afraid, nor be dismayed, for the Lord your God is with you wherever you go"*), 2 Timothy 1:7 (*"For God has not given us a spirit of fear, but of power and of love and of a sound mind"*), and Ephesians 6:10 (*"Finally, my brethren, be strong in the Lord and in the power of His might"*).

Yet in all these things we are more than conquerors through Him who loved us (Romans 8:37). And if we are Christ's, then we are Abraham's seed and heirs according to the promise (Galatians 3:29). Be ready, for we have stepped into our Jordan River and are crossing over into our Promised Land! Yes, we know that giants like unemployment, a government whose actions say they are not really for the people, home foreclosures, sickness, economic recession, and greed possess the land; but, we have been in bondage long enough, and no matter what nationality you are, if you are Christ's, then you are Abraham's seed and an heir according to the promise!

May our businesses establish, grow, and prosper! May our health prosper! May the relationships in our families prosper! May our friendships prosper! May we prosper in our work-places! May we prosper in our finances! May we prosper in our homes! May we prosper in our communities! May we prosper in our spirits! May our children prosper in their academics! May our children prosper in their spirits and personal walks with Christ! May we prosper in the Lord! May the establishing of the kingdom of God prosper! May we prosper in our Promised Land! May our prosperity be so in the mighty name of Jesus! Amen!

Nay, in all these things we are more than conquerors
through him that loved us (Romans 8:37).

Sweet Potato Casserole

Recipe

Sweet Potato Casserole

Ingredients:
4 eggs
2 cups granulated sugar
Two ¾ cup portions butter, softened
1 cup milk
1 tablespoon vanilla extract
6 sweet potatoes (boiled and mashed)
½ cup brown sugar
1/3 cup flour
2 tablespoons butter, softened
½ cup chopped pecans

Directions:

1. Beat eggs, granulated sugar, and ¾ cup (x2) of butter.
2. Mix in the milk and the vanilla extract.
3. Combine the mixture with the mashed sweet potatoes and spoon everything into a greased 2-quart casserole dish.

Topping

4. In a separate bowl, combine the brown sugar, flour, 2 tablespoons of softened butter, and pecans, mixing until crumbly.
5. Evenly sprinkle this mixture over the top of the sweet potato dish and bake at 350 degrees for 45 minutes.

Serves 8 or more.

Soul Food: *Soul Nourishing Devotionals and Recipies*
Volume 1

Nutrition Facts

Calories	248.5	Vitamin A	8.6 %
Total Fat	5.2 g	Vitamin B-12	0.0 %
Saturated Fat	1.2 g	Vitamin B-6	.3%
Polyunsaturated Fat	.3 g	Vitamin C	.8%
Monounsaturated Fat	.5 g	Vitamin D	0.0 %
Cholesterol	33.0 mg	Vitamin E	.3 %
Sodium	41.4 mg	Calcium	5.7 %
Potassium	87.5 mg	Copper	3.8 %
Total Carbohydrate	48.4 g	Folate	.4 %
Dietary Fiber	1.0 g	Iron	.6 %
Sugars	26.9 g	Magnesium	.2 %
Protein	3.1 g	Manganese	.9%
		Niacin	.3 %
		Pantothenic Acid	.2 %
		Phosphorus	1.3 %
		Riboflavin	3.3 %
		Selenium	3.1 %
		Thiamin	3.5 %
		Zinc	.7 %

And if ye [be] Christ's, then are ye Abraham's seed, and heirs according to the promise (Galations 3:29).

The Lord is not slack concerning His promise, as some count slackness, but is longsuffering toward us, not willing that any should perish but that all should come to repentance (2 Peter 3:9).

Winter Soul Food

His Promises

Second Peter 3:9 reads, *"The Lord is not slack concerning His promise, as some count slackness, but is longsuffering toward us, not willing that any should perish but that all should come to repentance."* Merriam-Webster's Dictionary defines the word promise as "a declaration that one will do or refrain from doing; a legally binding declaration that gives the person to whom it is made a right to expect or to claim the performance or forbearance of a specified act." Wow! God has bound Himself to the declarations of His Word and we, who His declarations have been made to, have the right to expect and claim performance by God according to His mighty Word! God's declarations in His Word are His promises. God promises to supply all of our needs (Philippians 4:19), He promises that His grace is sufficient for us (2 Corinthians 12:9), He promises to make a way of escape from temptation so that we are able to bear it (1 Corinthians 10:13), He promises us victory through our Lord Jesus Christ (1

81

Corinthians 15:57), He promises that all things work together for the good to those who love Him (Romans 8:28), He promises eternal life to His sheep that hear His voice and follow Him (John 10:27 - 28), He promises that those He establishes and anoints He also seals with His Spirit in our hearts as a guarantee (2 Corinthians 1:21 - 22), He promises to never leave us nor forsake us (Hebrews 13:5), and He promises to be with us always – even until the end of the age (Matthew 28:20)!

God's Word is true and it will accomplish what it is set out to do (Isaiah 55:11). God's Word will not – let me rephrase that – shall not return to Him void! (Isaiah 55:11) Why? Because God is not a man that He should lie, nor the son of man that He should repent (Numbers 23:19). God does not lie. What He speaks has to come to pass. These are just some of God's promises, and we are in receipt of them and so many more each and every day!

So I ask, are we offering the fruit of our lips (which is praise) unto Him, no matter what our present circumstance may be? Are we giving thanks in all things? Even if the promise of wealth has not come yet, or the promotion has not come yet, or the raise has not come yet, or the deliverance has not come yet, or the new job has not come yet, or the family relationships have not gotten better yet, or your healing has not fully manifested yet, or your dream home has not come yet, or your ministry has not taken off yet, or your business is not flourishing yet, or your check has not come yet, are we yet blessing, giving thanks unto, and praising the Lord our God? He is still sovereign and worthy! No matter what the situation or circumstance may be, He is still great, wonderful, mighty, awesome, the great I Am, Counselor, all powerful, the Beginning and the End, and with God nothing will be impossible (Luke 1:37)! Hallelujah! Glory be unto the Lord our God forever!

Our heavenly Father knows what's best for us, and in His timing the manifestation will happen and you will not be premature to receive it! For some of us, God is patiently waiting for our repentance (2 Peter 3:9). This is just one more of God's wonderful promises we receive each day. To those on whom God is yet waiting, in the words of my spiritual mentor: God is qualifying you! People of God, when you receive the manifestation of His promises made directly to you, you have just qualified! Keep pressing, keep praising, keep praying, keep confessing the Word of God, keep speaking what you know God said he will do and watch it come to pass. Remember that 2 Peter 3:9 says it loud and clear: *"The Lord is not slack concerning His promise!"* If God said He will do it, He is going to do it!

Divine Chili

Recipe

Divine Chili

Ingredients:
2 lbs Jimmy Dean mild Italian sausage
1 pack McCormick mild chile seasoning
1 pack McCormick spicy chile seasoning
4 cans dark red kidney beans, undrained
2 (14.5oz) cans of diced tomatoes in the can, undrained
1 box of Ritz Crackers

Directions:

1. In a frying skillet, brown the Italian sausage; after all the meat has thoroughly browned, drain the fat.
2. In a deep pot, mix the dark kidney beans, and whole tomatoes on medium heat, stirring occasionally. Once a slight boil has been achieved, add the McCormick seasoning and Italian sausage.
3. Mix thoroughly and allow simmering for 25 - 30 minutes, stirring occasionally.
4. Your Divine Chile is ready to serve with Ritz Crackers (or any side item/cracker of your choice).

Serves 8 or more.

NOTE: Because you will be handling pork and for health safety reasons, be sure hot water and soap are immediately available after handling the meat for cleaning and to wash hands after touching the raw meat.

Nutrition Facts

Calories	624.3		Vitamin A	28.6 %
Total Fat	26.0 g		Vitamin B-12	0.0 %
Saturated Fat	8.7 g		Vitamin B-6	11.1 %
Polyunsaturated Fat	0.4 g		Vitamin C	58.8 %
Monounsaturated Fat	2.9 g		Vitamin D	0.0 %
Cholesterol	100.0 mg		Vitamin E	4.5 %
Sodium	2,168.2 mg		Calcium	19.6 %
Potassium	654.7 mg		Copper	13.2 %
Total Carbohydrate	53.8 g		Folate	7.2 %
Dietary Fiber	12.7 g		Iron	33.9 %
Sugars	8.3 g		Magnesium	8.0 %
Protein	40.4 g		Manganese	15.2 %
			Niacin	11.9 %
			Pantothenic Acid	4.0 %
			Phosphorus	9.4 %
			Riboflavin	7.3 %
			Selenium	2.4 %
			Thiamin	9.9 %
			Zinc	4.1 %

The Lord is not slack concerning his promise, as some men count slackness; but is longsuffering to us-ward, not willing that any should perish, but that all should come to repentance (2Peter 3:9).

My little children, let us not love in word or in tongue, but in deed and in truth (1 John 3:18).

Winter Soul Food

Be the Change

While talking with my wife one time (her God-given wisdom never ceases to amaze me), she mentioned a quote from the Indian philosopher Mahatma Gandhi: "Be the change you want to see in the world." She went on to discuss how we can apply this principle to many of life's situations, especially as men and women of God. For example: we can "be the positive change we want to see in our spouse," "be the positive change we want to see in our community," or "be the positive change you want to see in society." As I read this quote, thought about it, and asked the Holy Spirit for help concerning it, it came to me: be the change God wants to see in the world!

Lately we've seen and heard a lot about needed change in the U. S. and world. We've heard it in presidential campaigning. We hear it from our leaders, we hear it from our friends, we hear it from our parents, we hear it from our colleagues, and we hear it just about everywhere we go. We've heard that there needs to be a change in the way the U. S. economy operates, we've heard that the federal tax system needs to be completely restructured, we've heard that vehicle mileage per gallon needs to increase, we've heard that the gap between the rich and poor needs decrease, we've heard that the racism in our country needs to improve, we've heard that the oil consumption needs to be reduced, we've heard that emissions of ozone-depleting gases must decrease and the list goes on. We must recognize the common factor in these desired changes is that they are from man. These changes are hoped for in order to increase material possessions and social status, which are things of this world. Jesus says in Matthew 24:35, *"Heaven and earth will pass away, but My words will by no means pass away."* The things (material possessions, social and societal status, etc.) of this world will pass away. With the steadily increasing woes of our society, there is a desperate need for a Holy Spirit makeover. So I ask: what about the change needed in the people for the glory of God and the further establishment of His kingdom?

In these last days, we are witnessing what the Word of God speaks of. There are those people claiming to be Christ Jesus and deceiving many. There are wars, rumors of wars, and natural disasters. Jesus says in Matthew 24:5 - 8,

> *For many will come in My name, saying, "I am the Christ,"' and will deceive many. And you will hear of wars and rumors of wars. See that you are not troubled; for all these things must come to pass, but*

the end is not yet. For nation will rise against nation, and kingdom against kingdom. And there will be famines, pestilences, and earthquakes in various places. All these are the beginning of sorrows."

So I ask again: what about the change needed in the people for the glory of God and the further establishment of His kingdom? Colossians 3:8-14 gives us a clear guide as to how we can be the change God wants to see in the world. It reads,

But now you yourselves are to put off all these: anger, wrath, malice, blasphemy, filthy language out of your mouth. Do not lie to one another, since you have put off the old man with his deeds, and have put on the new man who is renewed in knowledge according to the image of Him who created him, where there is neither Greek nor Jew, circumcised nor uncircumcised, barbarian, Scythian, slave nor free, but Christ is all and in all. Therefore, as the elect of God, holy and beloved, put on tender mercies, kindness, humility, meekness, longsuffering; bearing with one another, and forgiving one another, if anyone has a complaint against another; even as Christ forgave you, so you also must do. But above all these things put on love, which is the bond of perfection.

1 John 3:18 gives us the most effective way to accomplish this. It reads, *"My little children, let us not love in word or in tongue, but in deed and in truth."*

In order to see anger, wrath, malice, blasphemy, and filthy language change to tender mercies, kindness, humility, meekness, longsuffering, forgiveness, and love, we must stop just speaking about it and start being about it. Be the change God wants to see in the world. Let your actions speak for you, thereby promoting the change that is needed in the world for the glory of God and further establishment of His kingdom!

My little children, let us not love in word or in tongue, but in deed and in truth (1 John 3:18).

Easy Peach Cobbler

Recipe
Easy Peach Cobbler

Ingredients:
1 box white or yellow cake mix
½ stick butter
2 cans peach filling
1 tablespoon sugar

Directions:
1. Preheat your oven to 375 degrees Fahrenheit.
2. Pour the peach filling into a deep Pyrex or casserole dish. Evenly spread the filling.
3. Next, pour the cake mix evenly on top of the peach filling (should be an even thin layer).
4. Cut the butter into thin slices over the top of the cake mix (completely covering the top of the cake mix).
5. Lightly sprinkle sugar on top (optional).
6. Place the cobbler in a preheated oven and bake it for 45 minutes.
7. Remove the cobbler and allow it to cool before serving.

Serves 8 or more.

Nutrition Facts

Calories	324.3	Vitamin A	14.0 %
Total Fat	9.3 g	Vitamin B-12	0.0 %
Saturated Fat	2.5 g	Vitamin B-6	0.0 %
Polyunsaturated Fat	1.5 g	Vitamin C	4.0 %
Monounsaturated Fat	1.5 g	Vitamin D	0.0 %
Cholesterol	0.0 mg	Vitamin E	0.0 %
Sodium	380.7 mg	Calcium	8.0 %
Potassium	0.1 mg	Copper	0.0 %
Total Carbohydrate	60.7 g	Folate	0.0 %
Dietary Fiber	0.0 g	Iron	0.0 %
Sugars	40.8 g	Magnesium	0.0 %
Protein	1.7 g	Manganese	0.0 %
		Niacin	0.0 %
		Pantothenic Acid	0.0 %
		Phosphorus	0.0 %
		Riboflavin	0.0 %
		Selenium	0.0 %
		Thiamin	0.0 %
		Zinc	0.0 %

For I, the Lord your God, will hold your right hand,
saying to you, 'Fear not, I will help you'
(Isaiah 41:13).

Winter Soul Food

Go Through

I pray that your labor and persevering has not been in vain, and that as you are delighting yourself in Him you are receiving the desires of your heart (Psalm 37:4).

Romans 5:1 - 5 says,

Therefore, having been justified by faith, we have peace with God through our Lord Jesus Christ, through whom also we have access by faith into this grace in which we stand, and rejoice in hope of the glory of God. And not only that, but also glory in tribulations, knowing that tribulation produces perseverance; and perseverance, character; and character, hope. Now hope does not disappoint, because the love of God has been poured out in our hearts by the Holy Spirit who was given to us.

In these last days, we are facing ubiquitous obstacles, test, trials, situations, and distractions on a local and global scale. Whether manifested in troubled relationships, monetary lack, the absence of forgiving hearts and apologetic people for wronging others, or natural disasters, these things are troubling for the body of Christ! These devices are serving as tools that pull us from the body of Christ. These devices are used to take our minds away from thanksgiving and remaining in Jesus to a place of worry and heartache over the things we have no control over. These devices are being used to promote more complaining and less thanksgiving. These devices are used to steer us off course from our divine destiny. These devices are being used by satan to steal, kill, and destroy what God has ordained for our lives.

All of the obstacles, trials, and tribulations that we have gone through, are going through, or will go through, have a common denominator: we will go through them! When it comes down to the broad spectrum of what we face day in and day out, we have something that we must rely on more today than yesterday and more tomorrow than today – prayer. *"Confess your trespasses to one another, and pray for one another, that you may be healed. The effective, fervent prayer of a righteous man avails much,"* (James 5:16). Steadfast prayer accompanied with unwavering faith is what it will take to stay the course!

Remember that it is by faith in the death, burial, and resurrection of Jesus Christ that we are saved. Therefore, having been justified by faith, we have peace with God through our Lord Jesus Christ, through whom also we have access by faith into this grace in which we stand, and rejoice in hope of the glory of God (Romans 5:1 – 2). And not only that, but also glory in tribulations, knowing that tribulations produce perseverance, which produces character, which produces hope. Now hope does not disappoint, because the love of God has been poured out in our hearts by the Holy Spirit who was given to us (Romans 5:1 - 5).

What's so amazing about these trials is that they are all working together for our good (Romans 8:28) and producing passionate patience that forges the tempered steel of virtue, keeping us alert for whatever God will do next (Romans 5:1 – 5 MSG). Through it all, the good and the bad, God says in Isaiah 41:13, *"For I, the Lord your God, will hold your right hand, saying to you, 'Fear not, I will help you.'"*

God is our refuge (Psalm 46:1), we are victorious through Jesus Christ (1Corinthians 15:57), the battle is not ours but God's (2 Chronicles 20:15), and NO WEAPON FORMED AGAINST US SHALL PROSPER (Isaiah 54:17)!

Good God! Grilled Steak

Recipe

Good God Grilled Steak

Ingredients:	1 (16oz) T-bone steak Per Person
	1 bottle Dale's steak seasoning
	Zip Lock bags
	charcoal (personal preference is fine) and Grill

Directions: **Day 1**

1. The day or night before you cook, rinse the steak with cold water and place it into a Zip Lock bag.
2. over the steak with the Dale's steak seasoning. You will only need to pour just enough to cover both sides of the steak. Close the Zip Lock bag and roll the steak side to side inside the bag.
3. Refrigerate the steak over-night.

NOTE: Because you will be handling raw beef and for health safety reasons, be sure hot water and soap are immediately available after handling the meat for cleaning. Make sure that you isolate the area from any other food or items so that you don't cross contaminate. Finally, PLEASE be sure to thoroughly clean the area with disinfectant and soap and water after you finish preparing the steak (this includes your hands).

Day 2

1. Make sure you scrub and clean your grill using a grill scrub brush, hot water, and mild soap. Rinse thoroughly after cleaning. Place the charcoal evenly on the base of the grill, lightly soak the charcoal with lighter fluid, and ignite.

NOTE: Exercise extreme caution when dealing with fire and fuel. Allow all the charcoal to gray over. Make sure your grill vents are open. Now you are ready to begin placing the steak on the grill.

2. Placed the amount of steak the grill can safely handle, close the hood and allow the steak to cook for 5 - 10 minutes before turning. Repeat on the other side, turning again after 5 - 10 minutes.

101

NOTE: Be sure that flames are not coming up out of the charcoal. If they are, close the hood until they subside.

3. At this time, take your Dale's Steak seasoning and lightly sprinkle approximately 1 tablespoon of liquid directly on the side of the steak that is facing up. Allow the steak to cook another 5 - 10 minutes before turning. Repeat on the other side. Flip one more time and allow both sides to cook for 5 - 10 more minutes on each side. The inside temperature of the center of your grilled chicken should be at least 150 degrees Fahrenheit for it to be well done. At this temperature, your steak is ready. Enjoy!

Nutrition Facts

Amount Per 1 Serving		Vitamin A	0.0 %
Calories	613.8	Vitamin B-12	226.0 %
Total Fat	20.6 g	Vitamin B-6	95.3 %
Saturated Fat	8.0 g	Vitamin C	0.0 %
Polyunsaturated Fat	1.5 g	Vitamin D	0.0 %
Monounsaturated Fat	9.1 g	Vitamin E	2.9 %
Cholesterol	176.9 mg	Calcium	1.4 %
Sodium	1,483.1 mg	Copper	19.7 %
Potassium	1,419.8 mg	Folate	7.9 %
Total Carbohydrate	1.0 g	Iron	92.2 %
Dietary Fiber	0.0 g	Magnesium	26.1 %
Sugars	1.0 g	Manganese	3.2 %
Protein	98.8 g	Niacin	90.7 %
		Pantothenic Acid	15.4 %
		Phosphorus	87.1 %
		Riboflavin	50.7 %
		Selenium	64.8 %
		Thiamin	33.3 %
		Zinc	111.0 %

For I, the Lord your God, will hold your right hand, saying to you, 'Fear not, I will help you (Isaiah 41:13).

Final Remarks

As the season change I pray Volume 1 of *Soul Food* has not only fed your spirit man, but also brought great satisfaction to your natural body. I present and serve this volume to you as an appetizer to prepare your Soul and your appetite for the next course of *Soul Nourishing Devotionals and Recipes.*

I pray that you are blessed by the Word of God, and that it sinks into the very depths of your being and nourish your soul in Jesus' name!

Be blessed!

Yours in Christ,

Daunte' S. Gibbs

References

1. Holy Bible, The New King James Version, Thomas Nelson Publishers, 1985.
2. Note: All scriptural references that are not from The New King James Version have the abbreviation of the Bible Translation from which it was obtained.
3. Holy Bible, New Living Translation, www.biblegateway.com, 2008.
4. Holy Bible, New American Standard, www.biblegateway.com, 2008.
5. The Message: The Bible in Contemporary Language, Eugene H. Peterson, Navypress, 2005.
6. Nutritional information calculations, http://recipes.sparkpeople.com/recipe-calculator.asp
7. Note: All nutritional information was calculated utilizing the above-referenced source. Each calculation is an approximation and is based on a percent daily value diet consisting of 2000 calories.

About the Author
Daunte Gibbs

Daunte' Simone Gibbs is a native of Huntsville, AL. He is the second of three children to Stephen Gibbs, Jr. and Wanda Mae Gibbs (1954 – 1988). He is married to Sharee' P. Gibbs, a wonderful and anointed woman of God. They have a son named Christopher. Daunte' attended and graduated from J.O. Johnson High School, May 1998. He attended and graduated from Alabama A&M University with a Bachelor of Science in Environmental Science, May 2002. After which, he attended and graduated from the University of Georgia with his Master of Science in Environmental Health, May 2004. Daunte' currently resides in Winder, GA where he works as a County Planner for the Barrow County, GA Department of Planning & Development and is the owner of Gibbs Divine Catering (www.gibbs-divinecatering.net).

Daunte' received and accepted his call into the Ministry of the Gospel of Jesus Christ in January of 2007 and after careful observation and confirmation from the Lord through Bishop M. D. Spires and Pastor Timothy McKibbins, Minister Daunte' S. Gibbs was licensed as a minister by the Church of Atlanta Lighthouse, August 2009. If asked to summarize who he is, the following is his answer: "I am a man of faith. I am meek. I am kind. I am independent. I am strong. I am affectionate. I am nurturing. I am vigilant. I am determined. I am a thinker. I am who God says I am. I belong to Christ Jesus, therefore I am Abraham's seed, and an heir according to the promise (Galatians 3:24). I am the head and not the tail; I am above only and not beneath...(Deuteronomy 28:13). I am called and chosen (Matthew 22:14 & 1Peter 2:9). I am a man of God. I am a child of the true and living God, and redeemed of the Lord! Amen!" When asked what his ministry goals are, Minister Daunte' S. Gibbs' answer is, "I just desire that God be proud of me."

To order additional copies of *Soul Food* or to find out about other books by Daunte Gibbs or Zoë Life Publishing, please visit our website www.zoelifepub.com.

Special discounts are available for ministry, retail, academic or fundrasing purposes.

Contact Outreach at Zoë Life Publishing:

Zoë Life Publishing
P.O. Box 871066
Canton, MI 48187
(877) 841-3400
outreach@zoelifepub.com